W0114254

A MILLION LITTLE MIRACLES
GUIDED JOURNAL

40 REFLECTIONS TO
AWAKEN WONDER

A Million Little Miracles

Guided Journal

MARK BATTERSON

MULTNOMAH

Multnomah
An imprint of the Penguin Random House Christian Publishing Group,
a division of Penguin Random House LLC
1745 Broadway, New York, NY 10019

waterbrookmultnomah.com
penguinrandomhouse.com

All Scripture quotations, unless otherwise indicated, are taken from the Holy Bible, New International Version®, NIV®. Copyright © 1973, 1978, 1984, 2011 by Biblica Inc.™ Used by permission of Zondervan. All rights reserved worldwide. (www.zondervan.com). The "NIV" and "New International Version" are trademarks registered in the United States Patent and Trademark Office by Biblica Inc.™ Scripture quotations marked (BSB) are taken from the Holy Bible, Berean Standard Bible, BSB is produced in cooperation with Bible Hub, Discovery Bible, OpenBible.com, and the Berean Bible Translation Committee. Scripture quotations marked (CSB) are taken from the Christian Standard Bible®, copyright © 2017 by Holman Bible Publishers. Used by permission. Christian Standard Bible® and CSB® are federally registered trademarks of Holman Bible Publishers. Scripture quotations marked (ESV) are taken from the ESV® Bible (The Holy Bible, English Standard Version®), copyright © 2001 by Crossway, a publishing ministry of Good News Publishers. Used by permission. All rights reserved. Scripture quotations marked (KJV) are taken from the King James Version. Scripture quotations marked (MSG) are taken from *The Message*, copyright © 1993, 2002, 2018 by Eugene H. Peterson. Used by permission of NavPress. All rights reserved. Represented by Tyndale House Publishers. Scripture quotations marked (NKJV) are taken from the New King James Version®. Copyright © 1982 by Thomas Nelson. Used by permission. All rights reserved. Scripture quotations marked (NLT) are taken from the *Holy Bible*, New Living Translation, copyright © 1996, 2004, 2015 by Tyndale House Foundation. Used by permission of Tyndale House Publishers, Carol Stream, Illinois 60188. All rights reserved.

Copyright © 2026 by Mark Batterson

Penguin Random House values and supports copyright. Copyright fuels creativity, encourages diverse voices, promotes free speech, and creates a vibrant culture. Thank you for buying an authorized edition of this book and for complying with copyright laws by not reproducing, scanning, or distributing any part of it in any form without permission. You are supporting writers and allowing Penguin Random House to continue to publish books for every reader. Please note that no part of this book may be used or reproduced in any manner for the purpose of training artificial intelligence technologies or systems.

MULTNOMAH and the Multnomah M colophon are registered trademarks of Penguin Random House LLC.

Some material is adapted from *A Million Little Miracles* by Mark Batterson, copyright © 2024 by Mark Batterson, first published in the United States by Multnomah, an imprint of the Penguin Random House Christian Publishing Group, a division of Penguin Random House LLC, in 2024.

Library of Congress Cataloging-in-Publication Data

Names: Batterson, Mark, author.
Title: A million little miracles guided journal : 40 reflections to awaken wonder / Mark Batterson.
Description: New York, NY : Multnomah, 2026. | Includes bibliographical references.
Identifiers: LCCN 2025008139 | ISBN 9780593192894 (hardcover) | ISBN 9780593192900 (ebook)
Subjects: LCSH: Miracles—Anecdotes. | Presence of God—Anecdotes. | Spiritual journals.
Classification: LCC BL487 .B38 2025 | DDC 231.7/3—dc23/eng/20250428
LC record available at https://lccn.loc.gov/2025008139

Printed in the United States of America on acid-free paper

1st Printing

First Edition

The authorized representative in the EU for product safety and compliance is
Penguin Random House Ireland, Morrison Chambers, 32 Nassau Street, Dublin D02 YH68, Ireland.
https://eu-contact.penguin.ie

BOOK TEAM: Editor: Drew Dixon • Production editor: Jessica Choi • Managing editor: Julia Wallace •
Production manager: Angela McNally • Copy editor: Lisa Grimenstein •
Proofreaders: Carrie Krause, Rachel Kirsch

Book design by Fritz Metsch

For details on special quantity discounts for bulk purchases, contact specialmarketscms@
penguinrandomhouse.com.

CONTENTS

HOW TO USE THIS JOURNAL

If you have read *A Million Little Miracles* and are familiar with its contents, this journal is for you. And if you have gone above and beyond to read the accompanying study guide as well, then this journal is *definitely* for you! Allow me to explain the structure of this book.

There are forty days in this journal. Why? Because so many transitions and transformations in Scripture happen during a forty-day process. You might have taken a forty-day prayer challenge or gone through one of the books of the Bible in forty days. This journal is a forty-day journey into the millions of miracles that are all around you.

The experience of working through the content over a period of forty days will help you cultivate a habit of thinking about God, your relationship with Him, and your place in His wondrous world. But listen, there is no exact right way to work through this journal, so don't sweat it if it takes you a little—or a lot—longer than forty days. The point is to connect with God and grow in gratitude.

Rather than acting as a study guide for *A Million Little Miracles*, this journal gives you an opportunity to write down and record some of your unique thoughts and feelings. "Until it's on paper," said Sir John Hargrave, "it's vapor."[1]

Are you taking things for gratitude or are you taking things for granted? When was the last time you felt childlike wonder? What are some of your favorite parts of God's creation?

These are some of the questions you'll reflect on as you work through this journal.

Each day is divided into four sections. In the first section, there will be a Bible passage along with a question to prompt your writing. The second and third sections will include more questions along with quotes from the book. There is no right or wrong way to answer the questions. This is your journal, so write down whatever you want! The key is to put your thoughts onto paper. In the last section of each day, you are encouraged to think or do something differently. Call it an action step.

The goal of this journal is to help you experience God's miracles in a new and fresh way. God is "able to do immeasurably more than all we ask or imagine, according to his power that is at work within us" (Ephesians 3:20). My hope is that the eyes of your heart will be opened anew to the God who is bigger than big, closer than close, and gooder than good. And as you're experiencing this, you are writing down your thoughts along the way!

So grab a pen or a pencil and let's begin!

A MILLION LITTLE MIRACLES
GUIDED JOURNAL

HOLY CURIOSITY

---

*From the moment of conception until the day death
knocks on our door, life is more mysterious and
miraculous than we can imagine.*

—*A Million Little Miracles*

Take a breath.

Do you sense the miracle that is your life?

Look at the world.

Take note of the many strange and mysterious things around you.

What if you chose to be like Albert Einstein and never lose a "holy curiosity"? Do you have any holy curiosities? If not, try to come up with a few and list them here.

_____

_____

_____

_____

_____

_____

*Who is like you, O LORD, among the gods?
Who is like you, majestic in holiness,
awesome in glorious deeds, doing wonders?*

—EXODUS 15:11, ESV

There never has been and never will be
anyone like you. That's not a testament to you.
It's a testament to the God who created you.

—*A Million Little Miracles*

What makes you special and unique? Celebrate the person
God made you to be.

_____

_____

_____

_____

_____

_____

_____

_____

_____

_____

_____

_____

Every good and perfect gift is from above, coming
down from the Father of the heavenly lights, who does
not change like shifting shadows.

—JAMES 1:17

There are only two ways to live your life.
One is as though nothing is a miracle.
The other is as though everything is a miracle.

—Albert Einstein[1]

Which way are you living? When was the last time you felt a childlike wonder for ordinary miracles? Are you taking them for granted or for gratitude?

Think for a moment about God's miracles and wonders. Thank God for these amazing gifts.

_____

_____

_____

_____

_____

_____

_____

_____

_____

_____

_____

_____

_____

Every day we experience millions of little miracles, like the last breath you took and this morning's sunrise.

Ask yourself these questions today:

Is your God getting bigger or is your god getting smaller?
Is your understanding of God's power expanding or
    contracting?
How about God's love? His grace?

_____

_____

_____

_____

_____

_____

_____

_____

_____

_____

_____

_____

How much happier you would be, how much more of you there would be, if the hammer of a higher God could smash your small cosmos.

—G. K. CHESTERTON[2]

BAPTISM BY NATURE

You don't have to go far to find a million little miracles.
All it takes is a two-foot field trip. All you have to do is
go outside, look up, and count the stars.

—*A Million Little Miracles*

John Muir was a student of Scripture and a student of nature. He believed in baptism by water and by fire, but he also believed in baptism by nature. "Nature has always something rare to show us," he said.[1]

When was the last time you truly feasted your senses on the sights, sounds, and smells of earth, wind, and snow? List any of those moments.

_____

_____

_____

_____

_____

_____

_____

Methinks that the moment my legs begin to move, my
thoughts begin to flow.

—HENRY DAVID THOREAU[2]

The Lord took Abram outside and said to him,
"Look up into the sky and count the stars if you can.
That's how many descendants you will have!"

—Genesis 15:5, NLT

One minute Abram was in his tent, and the next he was outside hearing God tell him to look up and count the stars.

The sky was the limit for Abram.

What do you experience when you step outside and look at the sky? What are your thoughts when you stare at the stars?

_____

_____

_____

_____

_____

_____

_____

_____

_____

_____

_____

When we get outside the tent, it's easier to think outside the box. We start noticing everyday miracles.

—*A Million Little Miracles*

If you want to experience miracles,
sometimes it's as simple as introducing
a change of pace or a change of place.

—*A Million Little Miracles*

It is easy to fall into a routine. When was the last time you changed yours? Many new revelations happen when we change our routines! A small change can make a big difference!

This is the formula I live by:

Change of pace + change of place = change of perspective

What are some ways you can change your routine?

_____

_____

_____

_____

_____

_____

_____

_____

_____

_____

God likes to sanctify our expectations by supersizing them. That's exactly what He did with Abram. God gave him a night-light—a visual reminder of both his history and his destiny.

What are some of the visual reminders God has given you that display His greatness? Look for some of them today!

Don't turn a blind eye to the everyday miracles that surround you!

_____

_____

_____

_____

_____

_____

_____

_____

_____

_____

_____

When we lose touch with nature, we lose touch with nature's God.

—*A Million Little Miracles*

ASK THE EARTH
AND IT WILL TEACH YOU

I used to feel tremendous social pressure to be *interesting*.
I have since discovered, that's not how you win friends
and influence people. The key is to be *interested*. You have
to cultivate a non-anxious curiosity about other people,
and the master key is questions.

—*A Million Little Miracles*

George Washington Carver embodied the idea of holy curiosity. Born a slave, Carver became one of the greatest chemists and agronomists the world has ever known. His life verse was Job 12:7–8:

> But ask the animals, and they will teach you,
>   or the birds in the sky, and they will tell you;
> or speak to the earth, and it will teach you,
>   or let the fish in the sea inform you.

Carver would take long prayer walks through the woods early in the morning. Nature was the place where he would commune with God.

Consider some simple ways you could get out into nature. This could be as simple as walking outside your front door each day or making time for a walk in the park once a week.

The singing birds, the buzzing bees, the opening flower,
and the budding trees, along with other forms of animate
and inanimate matter, all have their marvelous creation
story to tell each searcher for truth.

—George Washington Carver[1]

What stories have you found outside in God's creation?
Where can you look for those?

_____

_____

_____

_____

_____

_____

_____

_____

_____

_____

_____

_____

Creation is God's cabinet of curiosities. It's full of mysteries and miracles.

—*A Million Little Miracles*

If you had a personal Mount Rushmore, like the four photographs that hang in my office, whose pictures would you hang? Who left their fingerprints on your soul? Who believed in you more than you believed in yourself?

—*A Million Little Miracles*

Think of your own personal Mount Rushmore and list the people who have influenced your life. Who can you leave your fingerprints on? Who can you choose to believe in?

_____

_____

_____

_____

_____

_____

_____

_____

_____

_____

_____

_____

_____

_____

_____

Do you carry a childlike sense of wonder? Or do you find yourself sleeping your way through life, unaware of the miracles all around you?

All you have to do is go outside.

So today, go outside. It doesn't matter when or where.

Just go.

_____

_____

_____

_____

_____

_____

_____

_____

_____

_____

_____

_____

_____

_____

Where do we find awe? The answer is *anywhere*!
                              —*A Million Little Miracles*

GOOSEBUMPS

*The feeling of awe is one of God's greatest gifts
and comes in lots of shapes and sizes.*

—*A Million Little Miracles*

When was the last time you felt awe—that feeling that comes from being in the presence of something vast? A feeling that can be triggered by things both large and small.

Awe defies definition. We may not always be able to find the words to describe it, but it is unmistakable when we experience it.

So, what experiences produce feelings of awe in your life? List some examples.

Be still, and know that I am God.

—PSALM 46:10

Mystery is immeasurable beauty. Mystery is
inexhaustible grace. Mystery is incalculable love.

—*A Million Little Miracles*

The psalmist said, "Magnify the LORD with me; let us exalt His name together."[1] How do we do that? We have to allow room for unknowable mysteries.

What are some unknowable mysteries in your life?

_____

_____

_____

_____

_____

_____

_____

_____

_____

_____

_____

_____

_____

_____

One of the secrets to faith is to always see
your life *against an infinite horizon.*

—Karl Rahner[2]

When was the last time you had goosebumps? What gives
you goosebumps?

Give thanks for those things by writing them down.

_____

_____

_____

_____

_____

_____

_____

_____

_____

_____

_____

_____

Goosebumps can be produced by kissing and by music,
but the most common type of goosebumps are those
caused by wonder.

—*A Million Little Miracles*

Today look for something that will fill you with awe and make you feel alive. Go outside. Climb a tree. Look up at the stars. Get lost in nature.

Maybe you need to change your routine. Do something new. Go somewhere different.

If you want to experience miracles, sometimes it's as simple as introducing a change of pace or a change of place.

There are a million little miracles right under your feet. All you have to do is take off your shoes!

—*A Million Little Miracles*

DAY 5

NEOTENY

Adults are obsolete children.

—Dr. Seuss[1]

I love the word *neoteny*. This zoological term refers to the retention of youthful qualities into adulthood. These qualities include characteristics often attached to youth, like curiosity, warmth, and playfulness.

How many childlike attributes do you carry around with you? Write down a few of them. If you can't think of any, then what are some youthful characteristics you would love to possess? Fearlessness? Eagerness? Energy?

Throughout the Bible, we see God's sense of playfulness. Psalm 104:25–26 is one example:

> There is the sea, vast and spacious,
>> teeming with creatures beyond number—
>> living things both large and small.
> There the ships go to and fro,
>> and Leviathan, which you formed to frolic there.

What comes to mind when you think about God? Do you see His sense of playfulness in your life? Below and on the following pages, write down moments when you can picture God smiling at something happening in your life.

Whether we're playing with Legos, playing games,
or playing music, God takes joy in our enjoyment.
It's a reflection of His playful personality, which we
greatly underestimate. In the words of C. S. Lewis,
"Joy is the serious business of Heaven."[2]

—*A Million Little Miracles*

It's never too late to become who you might have been.
The key? To become like Christ is to become like
a little child, and to become like a little child
is to recapture the sacredness of play.

—*A Million Little Miracles*

What are some ways you can recapture the sacredness of play
in your life?

_____

_____

_____

_____

_____

_____

_____

_____

_____

_____

_____

_____

_____

I still look at the world with uncontaminated wonder.

—WALT DISNEY[3]

Imagine all the things associated with youth:

Curiosity
Playfulness
Eagerness
Warmth
Energy

How can you incorporate these qualities into your life today?

_____

_____

_____

_____

_____

_____

_____

_____

_____

_____

Time is measured in minutes.
Life is measured in moments.
All that stands between you and a million little miracles is your capacity for wonder.

—*A Million Little Miracles*

TOV

There are moments in life when it's nearly impossible not to praise God. You guessed it—that is *tov*. They are those out-of-body experiences when heaven invades earth. They can't be captured in words, and the memory of them gets better with time.

—*A Million Little Miracles*

At the end of each creation day, God had the same reaction: He "saw that it was good." The Hebrew word for good is *tov*. But *tov* isn't just good, it's as good as it gets. This is what *tov* encapsulates:

Unadulterated pleasure
Pure delight
Overwhelming awe
Unspeakable joy
Childlike wonder

Tov is the definition of all that is good and true and beautiful.

What are some of your favorite parts of God's masterpiece of creation? Praise Him as you write them down.

God saw all that he had made, and it was very good.

—GENESIS 1:31

What is it that attracts people to faith in God? . . .
It's beauty and creativity and mystery.

—*A Million Little Miracles*

Think of the *tov* that you have experienced in your own life.

What is the most beautiful thing your eyes have ever beheld? What is a moment when time stood still? When have you felt most alive? What is the best feeling you've ever had?

_____

_____

_____

_____

_____

_____

_____

_____

_____

_____

_____

_____

Beauty will save the world.

—FYODOR DOSTOEVSKY[1]

Tov is the creativity of God that gives expression
to the goodness of God.

—*A Million Little Miracles*

What are those out-of-body experiences you've had when heaven invades earth? Those moments that can't be captured with words, where the memory of them gets better with time?

Try to capture them in words here. If it helps, draw a picture.

_____

_____

_____

_____

_____

_____

_____

_____

_____

_____

_____

_____

_____

At the end of each creation day, God took delight at His own creation. It's almost like He stepped back from the unveiling of His own masterpiece and said, "I outdid Myself, if that were possible!"

God wants us to continually rediscover how big, how close, and how good He really is.

Make it your goal to end the day the way God did: by taking delight in the work of your hands. This way, your life will become what it's truly meant to be—a daily delight.

God is most glorified in us when we delight in Him. We glorify God by enjoying God and all that He has made. We worship God by exploring, by naming, by stewarding, and, yes, by enjoying His creation.

—*A Million Little Miracles*

KABASH

What are we really *doing when we're doing what we're doing? It's so easy to learn* how *and forget* why!

—*A Million Little Miracles*

The Genesis Commission God gave to Adam and Eve is an invitation to exploration: "Be fruitful and increase in number; fill the earth and subdue it. Rule over the fish in the sea and the birds in the sky and over every living creature that moves on the ground" (Genesis 1:28).

The Hebrew word for subdue is *kabash*. This means to bring something under control that was out of control.

In relationship to creation, *kabash* has broad applications and implications. It's innovating and renovating; it's curating and cultivating.

What does it mean to subdue the earth? Write down some thoughts.

When an artist paints a picture, she is kabashing colors.
When a songwriter makes music, he is kabashing notes.
When an author writes a book, she is kabashing letters.

—*A Million Little Miracles*

Every one of us subdues something in our own unique way.
We all bring order to chaos. Every profession gives room for
good things to run wild.

So what do you *kabash* in your life?

_____

_____

_____

_____

_____

_____

_____

_____

_____

_____

The more I considered Christianity, the more I found
that while it had established a rule and order, the chief
aim of that order was to give room for good things to
run wild.

—G. K. CHESTERTON[1]

Have you ever considered that the same God
who crafted the universe with His voice
crafted furniture with His hands?

—*A Million Little Miracles*

What are ways you can see God bringing order out of chaos?
What biblical examples are there? What about current examples?

What are ways you can worship God through *kabash*?

_____

_____

_____

_____

_____

_____

_____

_____

_____

_____

_____

_____

_____

_____

_____

Nature caused King Solomon to come alive. There was nothing that the king didn't find endlessly interesting, nothing that didn't pique his holy curiosity. He wrote what sounds like a manifesto in Proverbs 25:2:

> It is the glory of God to conceal things,
>   but the glory of kings is to search things out. (ESV)

What can you go out and explore today?
How can you *kabash* God's glory?

The earth is God's playground, and we are God's playfellows.

—*A Million Little Miracles*

KEDUSHAH

Worship is when and where and how heaven invades earth!
Worship sets the stage for a million little miracles.
—*A Million Little Miracles*

In Judaism, different prayers entail different postures. One prayer is called the *kedushah*. It includes a recitation of Isaiah 6:3:

Holy, holy, holy is the LORD Almighty;
the whole earth is full of his glory.

When was the last time you clapped for the Creator?
When was the last time you gave God a standing ovation?
List some of those moments here.

There is a very fine line between taking things for
gratitude and taking things for granted. Once we cross
the line, a million little miracles are lost on us.

—*A Million Little Miracles*

Why do we take so many miracles for granted?
    Why don't we give God more standing ovations?
    List all the miracles in your life that deserve a standing O.

_____

_____

_____

_____

_____

_____

_____

_____

_____

_____

Bravo, GOD, bravo!
    Gods and all angels shout, "Encore!"
In awe before the glory,
    in awe before God's visible power.
Stand at attention!
    Dress your best to honor him!

—PSALM 29:1–2, MSG

The beginning of our happiness lies in the understanding
that life without wonder is not worth living. What we
lack is not a will to believe but a will to wonder.

—Abraham Heschel[1]

How do we live in a spirit of "radical amazement," as Abraham Heschel called it?[2]

What are ways you can find yourself radically amazed today?

_____

_____

_____

_____

_____

_____

_____

_____

_____

_____

_____

_____

_____

_____

How much are you enjoying God?
That's a pretty good measure of spiritual maturity.

—*A Million Little Miracles*

The chief end of man is to glorify God and enjoy Him forever.[3]
So go out and enjoy Him!

Don't take anything for granted.

Remember that everything is *awesome*!

_____

_____

_____

_____

_____

_____

_____

_____

_____

_____

_____

_____

_____

_____

THE INFINITUDE OF GOD

Show me the size of your dream, and I'll show
you the size of your God. God makes big people
by giving them big dreams.

—*A Million Little Miracles*

How big is your God?

Are you like Abram, who God told to "Look up"?[1]

Our biggest problem is our small view of God. We stay inside instead of going outside. We look down instead of looking up. We count our problems instead of counting the stars.

Consider Isaiah 66:1:

This is what the LORD says:

> "Heaven is my throne,
>   and the earth is my footstool."

Look up at the sky at night. Do you believe that God is bigger than everything you can see above you?

Reflect for a few moments on the greatness of God.

I'm often overwhelmed by situations I can't control and problems I can't solve. I'm overwhelmed by God-sized dreams that are beyond my ability, beyond my resources.

—*A Million Little Miracles*

What situations and problems are you overwhelmed with? Do you carry God-sized dreams that feel beyond your ability and resources? Write them down on this page.

_____

_____

_____

_____

_____

_____

_____

_____

_____

_____

_____

Because God's nature is infinite, everything that flows out of it is infinite also . . . How completely satisfying to turn from our limitations to a God who has none.

—A. W. TOZER[2]

Caleb tried to quiet the people as they stood before
Moses. "Let's go at once to take the land," he said.
"We can certainly conquer it!"

—Numbers 13:30, NLT

Think of Caleb's confidence in the character and promises of
God when he saw the giants in the promised land. Now think
back to all those situations and problems you listed on the
previous page.

Then pray this prayer: "It's bigger than me, Lord, but it's
not bigger than you!"

List those God-sized dreams again. What miraculous
things can happen in your life that will bring God all the
glory? What dreams are destined to fail without divine inter-
vention or guidance?

_____

_____

_____

_____

_____

_____

_____

_____

_____

We will never fully grasp the incomprehensible mystery of God. Even eternity won't be long enough to discover all that God is or praise Him for all that He has done.

Look for ways to grasp more of that mystery today.

Seek to discover God's delight in everything you do!

_____

_____

_____

_____

_____

_____

_____

_____

_____

_____

_____

_____

The Hound of Heaven never gives up on us, never stops wooing, never stops pursuing. All we have to do is turn around, and when we do, we discover a God with arms wide open.

—*A Million Little Miracles*

THE ADJACENT POSSIBLE

> The metanarrative of the Gospels is Jesus
> exercising His authority. Over what? Over everything.
> How did He do it? One miracle after another.
>
> —*A Million Little Miracles*

There's a concept introduced by Stuart Kauffman called the *adjacent possible*. It's a thing made possible by something else. He used it as a biological principle, but I like to apply it to theology.

Think of all the miracles Jesus did. List as many as you can in the following space.

Each points to the adjacent possible. When He walked out of the tomb on the third day, all bets were off.

Jesus looked at them and said, "With man this is impossible, but not with God; all things are possible with God."

—MARK 10:27

Impossible situations set the stage
for God's most amazing miracles.

—*A Million Little Miracles*

Imagine working in a skyscraper without the invention of an elevator.

Picture living in Florida without the creation of an air conditioner.

Visualize a chocolate chip cookie without an oven being invented.

It's impossible, right? Or at least, a lot less fun!

What are some special things in your life that were made possible because of something else?

_____

_____

_____

_____

_____

_____

_____

_____

_____

_____

_____

Miracles earn compound interest. You steward the miracle by believing God for even bigger, even better miracles.

—*A Million Little Miracles*

Sometimes we wait for miracles to happen, but we don't thank God for partial miracles—the "smaller" ways God guides, provides for, and cares for us each day. Think of all the partial miracles that have happened in your life and thank God for those.

_____

_____

_____

_____

_____

_____

_____

_____

_____

_____

_____

_____

Jesus *is* the adjacent possible! He is bigger than any impossible situation you may find yourself in.

_____

_____

_____

_____

_____

_____

_____

_____

_____

_____

_____

_____

_____

_____

_____

Everyone wants a miracle. Of course, no one wants to be in a situation that necessitates one! But you can't have one without the other.

—*A Million Little Miracles*

REALITY DISTORTION FIELD

It's impossible only until it isn't.

—*A Million Little Miracles*

How often do we say or believe that something is impossible?

How many times do we resemble Moses after God called him to deliver Israel out of Egypt? We tell God that we can't do something, that it's impossible.

What are some things in your life that you have felt are impossible for you?

God said to Moses, "I AM WHO I AM."

—EXODUS 3:14

Faith is taking the first step before God reveals the second step. If doubt is letting our circumstances get between us and God, faith is putting God between us and our circumstances.

—*A Million Little Miracles*

There are no limits on what God can do. He is an ever-present help in time of need.[1] He is the same yesterday, today, and forever.[2] He is I Am Who I Am.[3]

Write down all the ways God has been an ever-present help in your life. List things He has done in the past, things He is doing in the present, and what you pray He will do in the future.

_____

_____

_____

_____

_____

_____

_____

_____

_____

With the Lord a day is like a thousand years, and a thousand years are like a day.

—2 PETER 3:8

No power on earth or in hell can conquer the Spirit of
God in a human spirit, it is an inner unconquerableness.
—Oswald Chambers[4]

A reality distortion field is a force field. It's refusing to accept
limitations.

What would your life look like if you lived every day with
a reality distortion field?

_____

_____

_____

_____

_____

_____

_____

_____

_____

_____

_____

_____

_____

_____

The presence of God is one of those mysteries we take for granted. We don't miss it until we can't feel it.

The good news is, we don't have to manufacture miracles.

If you want to walk on water, you must get out of the boat.[5]

So how are you going to walk on water today?

_____

_____

_____

_____

_____

_____

_____

_____

_____

_____

_____

_____

_____

Faith is seeing the invisible and hearing the inaudible.
—*A Million Little Miracles*

GOD WINKS

Seeking God is the adventure that never ends!
—*A Million Little Miracles*

Do you find yourself overawed and overjoyed by the God who is bigger than big? Or do you find yourself still wrestling with doubts? If it's the latter, welcome to the club! That means you're human!

Now that you're twelve days into this journal, share some of the awe and joy you have discovered in God. Then describe some of the doubt you still carry.

We never reach a finish line when it comes to faith. We never arrive. Don't let that discourage you from seeking God!

"'If you can'?" said Jesus. "Everything is possible for one who believes."

Immediately the boy's father exclaimed, "I do believe; help me overcome my unbelief!"

—MARK 9:23–24

Every attribute of God is infinitely complex.

—A Million Little Miracles

Think of the infinitude of God. He can't be reduced to time or space, to numbers or letters.

God's love knows no limits. Neither does His power, His purposes, or His providence. His grace is sufficient for every situation we find ourselves in.

List all the ways God's grace is sufficient in your life.

Because He is infinite that love can enfold the whole created world in itself and have room for ten thousand times ten thousand worlds beside.

—A. W. TOZER[1]

Nothing is as simple as it seems.
Everything is more miraculous than we can imagine.

—*A Million Little Miracles*

One dimension of God's character is unpredictability. When you follow Jesus, expect the unexpected!

Some people might call these divine appointments. Or maybe they say it's when God winks.

How has God been unpredictable in your life? What God winks have you witnessed?

_____

_____

_____

_____

_____

_____

_____

_____

_____

_____

_____

_____

_____

_____

Scripture is full of head-scratchers like talking donkeys and sticks that turn into snakes. We know that God works in strange and mysterious ways. The unpredictability of God can be unsettling.

But at some point, we have to let go and let God. We need to trust our Creator.

Consider the miracles in your life. You can't manufacture miracles, but you don't have to!

Today, let God love you and grace you and heal you and empower you.

Let God repurpose you for His glory!

Jesus said, "If you hold to my teaching, you are really my disciples. Then you will know the truth, and the truth will set you free."

—JOHN 8:31–32

A SINGLE DROP OF WATER

---

*The mysteries and miracles of the human body
never cease to amaze.*

—*A Million Little Miracles*

Consider one of the great mysteries of life:

You!

It's mind-boggling to think that we all began as a single cell. The two hundred varieties of cells in our bodies are all so different. Think of how eye cells contrast with stomach cells.

We often take these microscopic miracles for granted. Think about some and write them down.

_____

_____

_____

_____

God's love is meteoric,
    his loyalty astronomic,
His purpose titanic,
    his verdicts oceanic.
Yet in his largeness
    nothing gets lost;
Not a man, not a mouse,
    slips through the cracks.

—PSALM 36:5–6, MSG

> It could be argued that inner space
> is more marvelous than outer space. It doesn't just
> defy imagination; it defies definition.
>
> —*A Million Little Miracles*

How many atoms are in a single drop of water? When I looked this up, I couldn't believe the answer!

An Italian scientist, Amedeo Avogadro, calculated the number of molecules in one mole of a substance. That number is $6.02214076 \times 10^{23}$.[1] We're talking a number in the sextillions!

Now think of how every snowflake is a beautiful and unique masterpiece.

Contrast the difference between outer space and inner space. Which is more mind-boggling and fascinating to you?

> Under the microscope, I found that snowflakes were miracles of beauty; and it seemed a shame that this beauty should not be seen and appreciated by others. Every crystal was a masterpiece of design and no one design was ever repeated.
>
> —WILSON BENTLEY[2]

God is great not just because nothing is too big.
God is great because nothing is too small.

—A Million Little Miracles

There is no detail of your life that God does not know. He knows the number of hairs on your head and every single tear you have shed.

Do you find it easy or difficult to believe that God knows you better than you know you? What does it mean that your name is written on the palms of His almighty hands?[3]

_____

_____

_____

_____

_____

_____

_____

_____

_____

_____

_____

_____

_____

_____

If a drop of water is more complex than we can imagine, how do we quantify God?

We don't.

God is incomprehensible.

His love is immeasurable, and His power is unimaginable. Yet He remains closer than close to us!

_____

_____

_____

_____

_____

_____

_____

_____

_____

_____

You made all the delicate, inner parts of my body
   and knit me together in my mother's womb.
Thank you for making me so wonderfully complex!
   Your workmanship is marvelous—how well I know it.
                                    —PSALM 139:13–14, NLT

GRATITUDE LISTS

---

*Until you have sufficiently counted your blessings,
you aren't ready for the next one.*
—*A Million Little Miracles*

When was the last time you counted your blessings? *Literally* counted them by numbering them?

How about taking a gratitude challenge? What would that look like for you? What sort of things do you typically take for granted that you can thank God for? Go ahead—think of as many as you can!

_____

_____

_____

_____

_____

_____

_____

_____

Rejoice always, pray continually, give thanks in all circumstances; for this is God's will for you in Christ Jesus.

—1 THESSALONIANS 5:16–18

Your gratitude list should be as unique as your fingerprint.

—*A Million Little Miracles*

How do you see the world? Each one of us sees only what we're looking for.

Are you looking for something to celebrate? You will always find it.

Are you looking for something to complain about? You will always find it.

What sort of things do you find yourself looking for every day? If there are more negative things, how can you change this?

_____

_____

_____

_____

_____

_____

_____

_____

_____

_____

Enjoy the little things. For one day you may look back and realize they were the big things.

—ROBERT BRAULT[1]

There is something about gratitude
that flips the switch on anxiety.

—*A Million Little Miracles*

Let's practice gratitude by starting a list right now! Keeping a list of things you can be thankful for helps train your brain to notice everyday miracles.

So dig deep and start counting your blessings. Don't just list the obvious ones or ones you've already written down in this journal. Remember—generic gratitude produces generic joy. Make your gratitude singular and specific to you!

_____

_____

_____

_____

_____

_____

_____

_____

_____

_____

_____

_____

_____

From sunrise to sunset, we have the opportunity to spiritually grow by giving God thanks. For what? For *everything*!

Today try to notice the constant miracles happening all around you and praise God for them. Use all your senses. Look and listen and lean into these limitless blessings!

_____

_____

_____

_____

_____

_____

_____

_____

_____

_____

_____

_____

_____

_____

Gratitude isn't getting what you want; it's wanting what you have. It's a growing awareness of and appreciation for a million little miracles.

—*A Million Little Miracles*

STUDY THE ANT

Camels have three stomachs, and they can shut their
nostrils during sandstorms.[1] Go ahead—try it.
Can't do it, can you?

—*A Million Little Miracles*

There's something to learn from everyone and everything.
That definitely includes animals! Almost anything you can do,
some type of animal can do better.

Owls hear better.

Eagles see better.

Kangaroos jump better.

Cheetahs run better.

Think of all the creatures that God created. Which ones
fascinate you the most? Why?

_____

_____

_____

_____

So God created the great creatures of the sea and every
living thing with which the water teems and that moves
about in it, according to their kinds, and every winged
bird according to its kind. And God saw that it was
good.

—GENESIS 1:21

There are at least twelve thousand species of ants
with a total population of twenty quadrillion—
that's 2.5 million ants per person.[2]

—*A Million Little Miracles*

When King Solomon said in Proverbs 6:6, "Go to the ant, you sluggard; consider its ways and be wise," this had universal application. We can learn something from every plant and animal on God's green earth.

Consider the fact that many ecosystems would collapse without ants.[3]

Consider that if bees were to go extinct, life as we know it would cease to exist.

What are things on God's green earth that you would like to learn something from? Why?

_____

_____

_____

_____

_____

_____

_____

Every ant knows the formula of its ant-hill, every bee knows the formula of its beehive. They know it in their own way, not in our way. Only humankind does not know its own formula.

—FYODOR DOSTOEVSKY[4]

You can't follow Jesus and be bored at the same time!
Never a dull moment when you follow in His footsteps.

—*A Million Little Miracles*

How does an eagle respond to being harassed by smaller birds? It flies higher.

How do buffalo deal with a coming storm? They run toward it.

I'll let you look up more details on that.

You need to live a life of holy curiosity. That curiosity should prompt you to learn more about your Creator.

Make a list of all the holy curiosities you can learn more about.

_____

_____

_____

_____

_____

_____

_____

_____

_____

_____

_____

_____

Are you curious about God's creation? Holy curiosity is a humble approach to everyone and everything. It's a learning posture that produces growth.

What questions can you ask today?

What answers will give you more insight about God?

_____

_____

_____

_____

_____

_____

_____

_____

_____

_____

_____

_____

_____

If you don't love God, it's because you don't *really* know God. How do I know this? Because *God* is love! True faith is always unlearning and relearning.

—*A Million Little Miracles*

STABS OF JOY

One of my rituals is clapping for trees
when they change color. They are too beautiful not to!

—*A Million Little Miracles*

When was the last time you marveled at something God made? That is as much worshipping God as singing in church.

We all have unique ways of worshipping the Creator. John Muir climbed trees during storms. George Washington Carver took prayer walks through the woods.

What's your unique way?

Write about how you can express praise at home, at work, and at play.

Open your eyes and there it is! By taking a long and thoughtful look at what God has created, people have always been able to see what their eyes as such can't see: eternal power, for instance, and the mystery of his divine being. So nobody has a good excuse.

—ROMANS 1:19–20, MSG

When C. S. Lewis was a young boy, his brother handed
him a biscuit tin filled with moss and decorated with
twigs and flowers. That simple little garden toy elicited
what Lewis called a "stab of Joy."[1]

—*A Million Little Miracles*

Have you had "stabs of joy" like the kind C. S. Lewis had in
his childhood?

For Lewis, that biscuit tin became holy ground, and it ini-
tiated a lifelong search for the source of that joy. Have you
been able to find that joy?

_____

_____

_____

_____

_____

_____

_____

_____

_____

I am a product of long corridors, empty sunlit rooms,
upstairs indoor silences, attics explored in solitude, dis-
tant noises of gurgling cisterns and pipes, and the noise
of wind under the tiles. Also, of endless books.

—C. S. LEWIS[2]

Did you know that trees communicate by releasing some of the same neurotransmitters as humans? Maybe that's why exposure to plants releases the feel-good neurotransmitter called dopamine.[3]

—*A Million Little Miracles*

What are new ways that you can worship God? Different ways to change your perspective on life? Creative ways to find "stabs of joy"?

Maybe it's a walk through the woods.

Maybe a visit to a museum.

Maybe a simple hike up a hill.

List some of those ways.

_____

_____

_____

_____

_____

_____

_____

_____

_____

_____

Every day we need to appreciate the simple pleasures in life, like a biscuit tin.

Sometimes we have to wait for them to come.

Sometimes they arrive out of nowhere like an unexpected gift.

Be on the lookout for stabs of joy today.

It's recognizing the good, the true, and the beautiful for what they really are—a million little miracles.

—*A Million Little Miracles*

ENJOY THE JOURNEY

> Have you seen the backside of a baboon? Don't tell me
> God doesn't have a sense of humor!
>
> —*A Million Little Miracles*

Have you ever had an experience that was terrifying when it happened but later on became incredibly awesome?

For me, one of these experiences was being held at gunpoint in Ethiopia. Another was camping at Awash National Park and witnessing wild animals in their natural habitat.

What's a terrifying-turned-awesome experience that you have had? What did you take away from it?

_____

_____

_____

_____

_____

_____

_____

_____

> Great is the LORD and most worthy of praise;
>   his greatness no one can fathom.
>
> —PSALM 145:3

I've met very few people who are possessed by a demon,
but I've met lots of people possessed by their possessions.
They don't own things. Things own them.
Friendly reminder? All the toys go back in the box
at the end of the game!

—A Million Little Miracles

When I was in Africa, I wrote in my journal something that
has become a rule of my life:

Don't accumulate possessions; accumulate experiences.

Experiences are the stuff that miracles are made of.

What are some rules of your life? Do you agree with my
rule?

_____

_____

_____

_____

_____

_____

_____

_____

_____

Quit living as if the purpose of life is to arrive safely at
death.

—MARK BATTERSON

The call of the wild is the intense yearning
to be immersed in nature.

—*A Million Little Miracles*

Do you know what cartographers call the blank spaces on maps?

Sleeping beauties.

They beckon us, like the call of the wild.

The instinct to explore is as old as Eden. What sleeping beauties are beckoning you?

_____

_____

_____

_____

_____

_____

_____

_____

_____

_____

_____

_____

_____

Where are you in your journey of life?

Are you accumulating possessions or experiences?

What places do you still have to explore?

What situations are waiting to fill you with joy?

One of my rules of life is to live in a way that is worth telling stories about.

—*A Million Little Miracles*

CHOOSE YOUR MIRACLE

> You can't prove or disprove intelligent design, but
> intelligent design makes more sense than
> some scientists are willing to admit.
>
> —*A Million Little Miracles*

Our origin story matters.

While Charles Darwin came to the conclusion that man bears the stamp of his lowly origin, I believe the exact opposite!

We are the image of God!

Life doesn't come from non-life. I believe in an infinite God who created the heavens and the earth out of nothing. Even if you don't believe in a Creator, you still need a cosmological starting point.

What are your thoughts about creation versus evolution?

_____

_____

_____

_____

_____

> You have made them a little lower than the angels
> and crowned them with glory and honor.
>
> —PSALM 8:5

You can't take God out of the equation of creation
and it not have ethical side effects.

—*A Million Little Miracles*

What happens when we take God out of the equation of creation?

What would it look like to live in a world that ultimately leads to a dead end of materialism, relativism, and nihilism?

_____

_____

_____

_____

_____

_____

_____

_____

_____

_____

_____

_____

Christians believe in the virgin birth of Jesus. Atheists believe in the virgin birth of the universe. Choose your miracle.

—GLEN SCRIVENER[1]

Every human shares 99.9 percent of the same DNA.[2]
That said, our 0.1 percent genetic variance makes
a huge difference, doesn't it?

—*A Million Little Miracles*

Each of us is unlike anyone ever! That diversity is a testament to God's creativity.

There never has been and never will be anyone like you!

Celebrate our Creator by writing down the most awesome aspects of your uniqueness.

_____

_____

_____

_____

_____

_____

_____

_____

_____

_____

_____

_____

_____

_____

You are fearfully and wonderfully made, so give God glory today!

Celebrate your 0.1 percent genetic variance and praise God for microscopic miracles!

_____

_____

_____

_____

_____

_____

_____

_____

_____

_____

_____

We recognize intelligent design when we see it. There had to be a clockmaker! If someone suggested that the clock started working in perfect synchrony, no intelligent design whatsoever, we would dismiss that person as illogical.

—SIR FRED HOYLE[3]

EXTRASENSORY PERCEPTION

Color is one of God's greatest creations!
—*A Million Little Miracles*

Just like every human being ever born, every color is truly unique. Each one absorbs and transmits different wavelengths of light. They also are a unique combination of chemicals.

What is your favorite color? Why do you like that color the best?

_____

_____

_____

_____

_____

_____

_____

_____

The twelve gates were twelve pearls, each gate made of a single pearl. The great street of the city was of gold, as pure as transparent glass.

—REVELATION 21:21

Everything will smell better, taste better, sound better,
feel better, and look better [in heaven].

—*A Million Little Miracles*

Most humans have three different cones in their eyes that di-
vide the colors our brains see into red, green, and blue.[1] But a
few rare people have one extra type of cone that allows them
to see a hundred million colors!

I wonder if we'll get a fifth cone in heaven that enables us
to perceive a billion colors. Or maybe a sixth, seventh, or hun-
dredth cone!

Imagine what you might be able to see in heaven. Name
some new colors. What other senses will become glorified?

_____

_____

_____

_____

_____

_____

_____

The only true voyage . . . would be not to visit strange
lands but to possess other eyes, to behold the universe
through the eyes of another, of a hundred others, to see
the hundred universes that each of them sees.

—MARCEL PROUST[2]

There is a reality that is more real
than anything we can perceive.

—*A Million Little Miracles*

What if your spiritual eyes were opened to everything happening around you? Imagine being able to see guardian angels! You would be able to discern the manifest presence of God!

What sort of reality can you picture happening in the spiritual realm we can't see? What would it be like to witness a million little miracles unfolding?

_____

_____

_____

_____

_____

_____

_____

_____

_____

_____

_____

_____

_____

The Spirit of God gives us extrasensory perception that allows us to hear the inaudible yet unmistakable voice of God. This is when we hear the still, small voice of the Spirit.

When was the last time you heard God's voice? What words of knowledge and wisdom did you learn from it?

_____

_____

_____

_____

_____

_____

_____

_____

_____

_____

_____

_____

_____

Many miracles are only perceived with eyes of faith that see between frames.

—*A Million Little Miracles*

HEAVENLY FREQUENCY

---

*God sang the universe into existence, and it's that song
that sustains the universe.*

—*A Million Little Miracles*

All around us, all the time, God is singing songs of deliverance. Creation sings in a four-part harmony in heaven, on earth, under the earth, and in the sea. It declares blessing and honor and glory and power to the Lord.

How do you imagine creation giving God glory? What is the sound of its praise? Write down any thoughts you have.

_____

_____

_____

_____

_____

_____

You will go out in joy
    and be led forth in peace;
the mountains and hills
    will burst into song before you,
and all the trees of the field
    will clap their hands.

—ISAIAH 55:12

Like laughter, music doeth good like a medicine!
—*A Million Little Miracles*

What sort of impact does music have on you? How does it make you feel? Do you agree with Thomas Carlyle when he said music "brings us near to the Infinite"?[1]

Share how music heightens your spiritual imagination.

_____

_____

_____

_____

_____

_____

_____

_____

_____

_____

_____

_____

_____

_____

_____

_____

Praise almost seems to be inner health made audible.
—C. S. LEWIS[2]

A great movie demands great music, and the same is true
of life. Worship is our soundtrack, and we need
look no further than the Psalms.

—*A Million Little Miracles*

What is the soundtrack to your life? Is worship a regular part
of that soundtrack? Why or why not?

_____

_____

_____

_____

_____

_____

_____

_____

_____

_____

_____

_____

_____

_____

We were created to worship. We can't *not* worship. One day our worship will be perfect. Revelation 21:4 states that there is a heavenly frequency where there is no more death or sorrow or crying or pain.

How can you find new ways in your life to worship God? In what ways can you get on God's wavelength? How will you seek to discern the still, small voice of the Spirit today?

_____

_____

_____

_____

_____

_____

_____

_____

_____

_____

_____

_____

_____

_____

When we worship, we are harmonizing with heaven.
—*A Million Little Miracles*

THE WONDER SWITCH

In Greek, the etymology of the word for "wonder" is the
same as the word for "miracle."[1] They are
two sides of the same coin.

—*A Million Little Miracles*

According to illusionist Harris III, all of us have a wonder switch, and we are born with that switch on.[2] Everything is awesome and our minds are endlessly creative.

Think back to your childhood. What were some of the most awesome things you ever experienced? Write about those.

_____

_____

_____

_____

The heavens declare the glory of God;
    the skies proclaim the work of his hands.
Day after day they pour forth speech;
    night after night they reveal knowledge.
They have no speech, they use no words;
    no sound is heard from them.
Yet their voice goes out into all the earth,
    their words to the ends of the world.

—PSALM 19:1–4

Sooner or later, one way or the other, the wonder switch is
turned off. All too often, it happens when we are
robbed of our childlike innocence.

—*A Million Little Miracles*

Is your wonder switch on or off?
    If it is off, what caused it to turn off?
    Write about that childhood innocence you once had.

We are born able to sing to birds and read the clouds
and see our destiny in grains of sand. But then we get
the magic educated right out of our souls. We get it
churched out, spanked out, washed out, and combed
out.

—ROBERT MCCAMMON[3]

Nothing glorifies God like childlike wonder.

—*A Million Little Miracles*

We all lose our innocence sooner or later. So how do we get it back?

All we have to do is consider the millions of little miracles that await us outside. Look up at the stars! Look down at the lilies!

What things can you do to reclaim your childhood wonder?

_____

_____

_____

_____

_____

_____

_____

_____

_____

_____

_____

_____

_____

_____

Thomas Carlyle said "worship is transcendent wonder, wonder for which there is now no limit or measure."[4]

Do you put limits and measures on your outlook in life?

_____

_____

_____

_____

_____

_____

_____

_____

_____

_____

_____

_____

If you want to recapture the wonder you had in your childhood, it starts with rediscovering everyday miracles. Reclaim the spark in your life and turn that wonder switch on!

You do you, but do it to the glory of God.

—*A Million Little Miracles*

THE DANDELION PRINCIPLE

Everything is more miraculous than we can imagine.
—A Million Little Miracles

At six feet four and more than three hundred pounds, G. K. Chesterton was a mountain of a man, yet he had an appreciation for little things. One day he was stopped in his tracks by a tiny little thing.

A dandelion.

The yellow flower proved to him that there was beauty in this broken world. With one look at the dandelion, Chesterton woke up to wonder. This event inspired him to seek out spiritual truth for the rest of his life.

What are the dandelions in your life? A person? A place? An experience? Write them down.

_____

_____

_____

_____

_____

Consider the birds of the sky: They don't sow or reap or gather into barns, yet your heavenly Father feeds them. Aren't you worth more than they?

—MATTHEW 6:26, CSB

There are a million little miracles hiding in plain sight.
Of that I'm sure. But we must "learn to look" from
different angles! When we do, we see
new dimensions of who God is.

—*A Million Little Miracles*

Have you tried to find miracles in your life? Have you tried looking from different angles?

Consider all the facets of your life: your family, your job, your friends, your neighborhood, your church, your passions. How can you view these from different angles to spot new miracles?

_____

_____

_____

_____

_____

_____

_____

_____

The object of the artistic and spiritual life was to dig for this submerged sunrise of wonder; so that a man sitting in a chair might suddenly understand that he was actually alive, and be happy.

—G. K. CHESTERTON[1]

There are ten thousand species of jellyfish—evidence
that God loves variety. Some are as small as
one-half millimeter in diameter.

—*A Million Little Miracles*

Can you see the miracle of God's creation in a jellyfish? At
first it looks like nothing more than a gelatinous mass, but
when you observe it closely, you will find a remarkable and
complicated structure.

What are other "jellyfish" in your life that you never pay
close attention to? Why might these not be as simple as you
think? How might actively acknowledging these things
change your perspective?

_____

_____

_____

_____

_____

_____

_____

_____

_____

_____

_____

"Consider the birds of the sky," [Jesus said.]
—Matthew 6:26, CSB

If I'm reading this right, Jesus was advocating bird-watching.
Birds have something big to teach us:

There is a heavenly Father who cares for us more than we
can imagine. The Father is always watching out for us.

Today, don't be anxious about anything.

Consider the dandelions.

Consider the jellyfish.

Consider Jesus speaking to you words that soothe your
soul.

Stars, birds, or flowers—nature is God's show-and-tell.
—*A Million Little Miracles*

IMAGINATION IS EVERYTHING

Imagination is not just part of the image of God,
but it's also the quintessence. As such, it's a superpower
unique to humankind.

—*A Million Little Miracles*

Think of all the amazing things humans have done.

We have built skyscrapers.

We have split atoms.

We have designed computers.

We can write poems, compose music, and produce films.

What is the most imaginative part about yourself? How do you use your God-given creativity?

_____

_____

_____

_____

_____

_____

_____

_____

For as [a man] thinketh in his heart, so is he.

—PROVERBS 23:7, KJV

The greatest mysteries in the universe are not "out there."
They're "in here." Where? They're housed within the
three pounds of gray matter contained within the
human cranium.

—*A Million Little Miracles*

Thoughts can create things. Humans are not just thinking be-
ings; we have the ability to think about how we think.

So how do *you* think? Do you find yourself being creative?
Contemplative? Problem-solving? How does your brain work?

_____

_____

_____

_____

_____

_____

_____

_____

_____

_____

_____

The human brain is the most complex single object in
the cosmos.

—JOHN LLOYD AND JOHN MITCHINSON[1]

> Like the Hebrew concept of kabashing creation,
> which we already explored, every human creation is
> conceived in the imagination.
>
> —*A Million Little Miracles*

Grasshoppers are a testament to God's creativity.

They can do a thirty-inch-long jump—that's twenty times their body length.[2]

They can jump three feet high.[3]

Their muscles have ten times the power of human muscles.

And they can sing their own unique song.

Have you ever looked at or listened to a grasshopper and marveled at God's creativity? What are other demonstrations of this?

_____

_____

_____

_____

_____

_____

_____

_____

_____

_____

Franz Kafka said that imagination does not require that you even leave your room; it involves no passport and has no borders.[4]

How can you use imagination in your life today? How can you allow it to create your own song and speak every language?

_____

_____

_____

_____

_____

_____

_____

_____

_____

_____

_____

_____

_____

_____

It's our God-given imagination that powers everything from rockets to romance. It's imagination that allows us to break through eight-foot ceilings.
                                    —*A Million Little Miracles*

IMAGINARIUM OF TEARS

The shortest verse in the Bible says, "Jesus wept."
It's only two words, but it speaks volumes. This is
the God who weeps when we weep.

—*A Million Little Miracles*

You matter. You matter more than the birds of the air and the lilies of the field. You matter more than you can imagine.

That's because you matter to God.

Do you believe that? Do you walk confidently knowing that you are precious in God's sight? Or do you battle hurt and loneliness on a daily basis?

Be honest and share your thoughts.

See, I have written your name on the palms of my hands.

—ISAIAH 49:16, NLT

Whether we're grieving the loss of a loved one
or shedding tears of joy, each tear is uniquely
precious to God.

—*A Million Little Miracles*

After examining his tears, Danish photographer Maurice Mikkers discovered the different microscopic patterns each drop produced. He created an art project called *Imaginarium of Tears* that reveals how, when tears are put under a microscope, they look like snowflakes—each one different from the rest.

This is another miracle that reminds us how fearfully and wonderfully we're made.

When was the last time you cried? Did you feel God's presence?

_____

_____

_____

_____

_____

_____

_____

Everyone should be able to share his or her tears. Because tears are stories. And stories connect us on a deeper level.

—MAURICE MIKKERS[1]

Every number has a name, every name has a story,
and every story matters to God.

—*A Million Little Miracles*

God knows every single joy and sorrow you carry.
What does the following verse mean to you?

You keep track of all my sorrows.
    You have collected all my tears in your bottle.
    You have recorded each one in your book. (Psalm
    56:8, NLT)

We all go through dark nights of the soul.

There are times when we might doubt our faith.

But remember that God is our refuge and strength. He is an ever-present help in trouble who sees every single tear we shed.

What are moments in your life when you felt sustained by the Spirit of God?

_____

_____

_____

_____

_____

_____

_____

_____

_____

_____

_____

_____

I know that God can sometimes feel a million miles away, but He is only a prayer away.

—*A Million Little Miracles*

THE LONELINESS EPIDEMIC

Spirituality is a team sport. Even Jesus had His disciples!
That is when and where and how iron sharpens iron.

—*A Million Little Miracles*

We were created for relationships. From the get-go, God said, "It is not good for the man to be alone."[1] Without healthy relationships, there are serious side effects.

What are the healthy relationships in your life? What about the unhealthy relationships? Consider the people in your life. Do they speak the truth in love?

The LORD God said, "It is not good for the man to be alone. I will make a helper suitable for him."

—GENESIS 2:18

When you find common ground at the foot
of the cross, it allows you to celebrate diversity
as evidence of God's creativity.

—*A Million Little Miracles*

Have you ever experienced loneliness? Or have you suffered church hurt? How has this affected your being a part of the church body? Do you find this easy or difficult?

Do you believe that our love for Christ can overcome any sort of tension or division we might have? Share your thoughts on this page.

Unity amongst dissimilar people is irrefutable evidence that God is in the house.

—DAVID GRIZZLE

Loneliness is epidemic these days.
Even in a crowd, some of us feel so alone.

—*A Million Little Miracles*

Think of your most recent church experience. Did you feel seen, heard, and loved by God? How about seen, heard, and loved by others? Why or why not?

_____

_____

_____

_____

_____

_____

_____

_____

_____

_____

_____

_____

_____

_____

_____

_____

There is one prescription for hurt that the writer of Hebrews penned: "Let us not neglect our meeting together, as some people do, but encourage one another" (10:25, NLT).

When two people pray together . . .

When a small group gathers . . .

When a congregation worships God corporately . . .

In all those cases, there is a supernatural synergy that happens.

_____

_____

_____

_____

_____

_____

_____

_____

_____

_____

_____

_____

The transformational power of community is one of God's most life-giving miracles—don't miss it.

—*A Million Little Miracles*

GOODER THAN GOOD

God is gooder than good—He is God Most Good.

—*A Million Little Miracles*

We've looked at how God is bigger than big and closer than close. Now let's look at how He is gooder than good.

Every miracle that has been mentioned in this journal is a manifestation of God's goodness. What is that called? Common grace.

When you hear the phrase "God's goodness," what does that mean to you? How would you define common grace? Write down your thoughts.

_____

_____

_____

_____

_____

_____

Do you despise the riches of His goodness, forbearance, and longsuffering, not knowing that the goodness of God leads you to repentance?

—ROMANS 2:4, NKJV

I have a theory: *To know God is to love God.*
—*A Million Little Miracles*

Do you know God? Do you love God?

People who reject God are rejecting a false conception of who God is—a God who is less than good.

What are false beliefs and narratives that you or others have believed about God? What is the truth about these false beliefs?

_____

_____

_____

_____

_____

_____

_____

_____

_____

_____

_____

_____

"Safe?" said Mr. Beaver; . . . "Who said anything about safe? 'Course he isn't safe. But he's good."
—C. S. LEWIS, *The Lion, the Witch and the Wardrobe*[1]

God's goodness is long-suffering. In other words,
God never gives up on us! It's not in His nature.
He is the God of second chances.

—*A Million Little Miracles*

Proverbs 6:16–19 describes the seven things God hates:

These six things the LORD hates,
Yes, seven *are* an abomination to Him:
A proud look,
A lying tongue,
Hands that shed innocent blood,
A heart that devises wicked plans,
Feet that are swift in running to evil,
A false witness who speaks lies,
And one who sows discord among brethren. (NKJV)

Why does God hate those things? Because He loves us
and is deeply invested in our flourishing!

Share your thoughts about God's holiness and hatred of
sin compared to His kindness and long-suffering.

_____

_____

_____

_____

_____

_____

_____

Our goal is to become men and women after God's own heart. So look at yours.

Does your heart break for the things that break the heart of God?

Does your heart beat for the things that cause God's heart to skip a beat?

Today, remember that the greatest miracles are the manifestations of God's goodness. "For from his fullness we have all received, grace upon grace" (John 1:16, ESV).

_____

_____

_____

_____

_____

_____

_____

_____

_____

The last thing God wants is a fear-based relationship. Yes, the fear of God is the beginning of wisdom.[2] But in Scripture, the fear of God is an expression of awe, not intimidation! The fear of God is wonder for which there are no words. You could even call it the wonder switch.

—*A Million Little Miracles*

A PROGRESSIVE REVELATION

From Genesis to Revelation, Scripture paints
a composite picture of who God is.

—*A Million Little Miracles*

Imagine a big book authored by more than forty people from every walk of life—farmers and fishermen, poets and prophets, a doctor, tax collector, and prime minister.

Picture these authors writing in prison cells and palace courts and wilderness caves.

Think of the gamut of human experience that book must cover. There is comedy and tragedy, history and mystery, romance and action-adventure, and even poetry.

Yes, I'm talking about the big book we call the Bible. It consists of sixty-six books written in three languages on three continents over a period of fifteen hundred years!

How incredible is that? Write down some thoughts on the marvel and mystery of holy Scripture.

_____

_____

_____

_____

_____

_____

_____

All Scripture is God-breathed and is useful for teaching, rebuking, correcting and training in righteousness,
so that the servant of God may be thoroughly equipped
for every good work.

—2 TIMOTHY 3:16–17

Regardless of how you summarize Scripture,
the plotline is a progressive revelation.

—*A Million Little Miracles*

Have you ever read the Bible from cover to cover? If not, why not make that a goal?

There is one inevitable, undeniable, and incontrovertible truth in the Bible: God is God, and we're not. Someday all of us will bow before the throne of God.

When you think of the Bible as one big book, what is the primary message you take away from it? What are the parts you know well and the parts you're curious about?

That God is good is taught or implied on every page of the Bible and must be received as an article of faith as impregnable as the throne of God.

—A. W. TOZER[1]

There are many ways to cliffnote Scripture.

—*A Million Little Miracles*

My spiritual father, Dick Foth, summarizes the Bible with four phrases:

God left His place.
He came to our place.
He took our place.
Then He invites us back to His place.

There are many ways you can summarize Scripture. You can categorize the covenants or the Bible's defining moments. I am not suggesting that understanding the CliffsNotes version of the Bible is sufficient; however, it is helpful to observe the big-picture story of the Bible.

Summarize Scripture in your own words.

_____

_____

_____

_____

_____

_____

_____

_____

From Genesis to Revelation, we see a composite picture of a good God. All throughout Scripture, we see the revelation of God's heart toward humankind.

If you've never read the Bible from cover to cover, start today. And if you have, continue diving into the holy Word!

At Bethlehem, He is God *with* us. At Calvary, He is God *as* us. At the empty tomb, He is God *for* us. At Pentecost, He is God *in* us.

—*A Million Little Miracles*

NAME ABOVE ALL NAMES

We have a natural tendency to create God in *our* image.
But when we filter our theology through our histories,
personalities, ethnicities, and idiosyncrasies, it's called
idolatry. That's when we've got to deconstruct and
reconstruct our internal image of who God is.

—*A Million Little Miracles*

As we said yesterday, from the first verse of Genesis to the last line of Revelation, Scripture paints a composite picture of who God is. But a common mistake is when we make God in our own image. We do this by cutting and pasting the character of God, leaving us with a caricature of God.

What is your picture of God? How do you view His character? Write down your description below.

_____

_____

_____

_____

_____

_____

_____

_____

_____

_____

_____

_____

" 'The Lord bless you
     and keep you;
the Lord make his face shine on you
     and be gracious to you;
the Lord turn his face toward you
     and give you peace.' "

So they will put my name on the Israelites, and I will
bless them.

—NUMBERS 6:24–27

God puts His name—Jehovah Tsidkenu—on us!
You, my friend, are the righteousness of Christ.

—A Million Little Miracles

One way we can grow spiritually is by getting to know the names of God. These names reveal God's character.

Did you know that there are 967 names for God in Scripture? Here are just a few:[1]

Jehovah Rapha—God our Healer
Jehovah Jireh—God our Provider
Jehovah Shalom—God our Peace
Jehovah Tsidkenu—God our Righteousness
Jehovah Nissi—God our Banner

Each new name we discover makes us hallow His name a little more. We shouldn't just know these names; we should try them on for size.

Look up other names for God and write down their meanings.

_____

_____

_____

_____

_____

Every Story in the Bible whispers His name.

—SALLY LLOYD-JONES[2]

The character of God is immutable—He is the same
yesterday, today, and forever. God is *Tov* forever and for
always. It doesn't get any gooder than God.

—*A Million Little Miracles*

The gospel of John shares seven "I Am" statements that reveal
the character of Jesus.

I am the Bread of Life.
I am the Light of the World.
I am the Gate.
I am the Vine.
I am the Good Shepherd.
I am the Resurrection and the Life.
I am the Way, the Truth, and the Life.[3]

What is your definition of each "I Am" statement here?

How do *you* describe Jesus Christ? What name do you give Him?

Always remember that Jesus is the answer to every question.

Jesus is the solution to every problem.

Jesus is the fulfilment of every promise!

Jesus is the dictionary in which we look up the meaning of words.

—EUGENE PETERSON[4]

GOODWILL TOWARD MEN

It's from the superabundance of His grace
that we have received blessing upon blessing.
That's how we go from glory to glory.[1]

—*A Million Little Miracles*

What is the very first thing God did after creating human-kind in His image?

He blessed them.

That is who God is. That is what He does. Blessing is God's most ancient instinct. Maybe that's why blessing is our deep-est longing.

Have you felt God's blessings in your life? List them here. If you haven't felt them, why do you think that is?

_____

_____

_____

_____

_____

For the LORD God is a sun and shield;
    the LORD bestows favor and honor;
no good thing does he withhold
    from those whose walk is blameless.

—PSALM 84:11

Blessing is your birthright.

—*A Million Little Miracles*

God is good. That simple and profound statement is what the Enemy has been trying to undermine since the beginning of time.

Before original sin, there was original doubt. The serpent planted a seed of doubt in Eve's heart. It was based on a false narrative that God was withholding good by keeping the tree of knowledge of good and evil off-limits.

Do you have doubts about God? Do you ever feel like God is withholding something good from you? Write down your thoughts.

_____

_____

_____

_____

_____

_____

_____

_____

The ultimate question is whether the doctrine of the goodness of God or that of the inerrancy of Scriptures is to prevail when they conflict. . . . The doctrine of the goodness of God is the more certain of the two.

—C. S. LEWIS[2]

The Enemy rarely engages in frontal assaults,
because they are too obvious.

—*A Million Little Miracles*

The Enemy always wants to make God seem less good. He wants us to second-guess the goodness of God.

Why do you think this is significant? How does the Enemy do this in subtle and small ways?

_____

_____

_____

_____

_____

_____

_____

_____

_____

_____

_____

_____

_____

_____

_____

The angels declared to the shepherds outside Bethlehem:

> Glory to God in the highest
> And on earth peace, goodwill toward men! (Luke 2:14,
> NKJV)

> Don't miss the significance of this declaration.
> God's will is goodwill.
> God's will is good, pleasing, and perfect.[3]
> Today remember God's goodness.

He who began a good work in you will carry it on to
completion until the day of Christ Jesus.

—PHILIPPIANS 1:6

THE LIFE LIE

If you want to change your life,
you have to change your story!
—*A Million Little Miracles*

For better or worse, you are the narrator of your story. So what story are you telling?

Are you telling the truth about yourself, or are you making up fiction?

We can create life lies where we fashion false beliefs around our lives. It's a form of self-sabotage. It's also an excuse we give ourselves to evade responsibilities.

This false belief turns into a false narrative that turns into a false identity that turns into a false reality.

Have you ever created life lies? What have been some of those false narratives and false realities?

Moses said to the LORD, "Pardon your servant, Lord. I have never been eloquent, neither in the past nor since you have spoken to your servant. I am slow of speech and tongue."

—EXODUS 4:10

If you're looking for an excuse, you will always find one!

—*A Million Little Miracles*

Moses is a classic case study of a life lie. When God called him to deliver Israel out of Egypt, he gave himself an excuse to evade responsibility. He told God he wasn't eloquent and that he was slow to speech. You gotta love God's response: "I will help you speak and will teach you what to say" (Exodus 4:12).

The irony was that Moses was bilingual, which was a pretty big deal back then. But like many of us, Moses was way more aware of his weaknesses than his strengths.

What are some of your strengths? As you think about the life lies you've had, write down the strengths God has given you to conquer them.

_____

_____

_____

_____

_____

_____

_____

_____

The greatest problems can never be solved, but only outgrown.

—CARL JUNG[1]

If you leave God out of the equation, good luck!

—*A Million Little Miracles*

Sometimes it's easy to give the Enemy more credit than he deserves. Yes, Lucifer is the father of lies, but he is only a fallen angel. He isn't omniscient or omnipotent. He plays mind games, but he can't read your mind. He doesn't know your future—but you know his!

Do you ever give the Enemy more credit than he deserves? If so, how? How can you take more responsibility for your mistakes?

_____

_____

_____

_____

_____

_____

_____

_____

_____

_____

_____

_____

We shouldn't be unaware of the devil's schemes. We've got game film on the Enemy going all the way back to the Garden of Eden, and his tactics haven't changed. He usually doesn't propagate bald-faced lies but rather peddles half-truths.

Don't let seeds of doubt take root.

If you have any life lies that are growing inside, get rid of them today!

_____

_____

_____

_____

_____

_____

_____

_____

_____

_____

_____

_____

_____

If you let those lies take root, you start living the wrong story.

—*A Million Little Miracles*

ORDER OUT OF CHAOS

———————

Free will is the free radical in the algorithm of life.
—*A Million Little Miracles*

If God is good, why do bad things happen to good people?

If God is all-powerful, why is there pain and suffering?

Have you ever asked yourself those questions? This is one of the primary reasons people lose faith: They see suffering as evidence against the existence of God.

What are your answers to those questions?

_____

_____

_____

_____

_____

_____

_____

_____

To all who mourn in Israel,
    he will give a crown of beauty for ashes,
a joyous blessing instead of mourning,
    festive praise instead of despair.

—ISAIAH 61:3, NLT

> We tend to complain about what's wrong rather than
> celebrate what's right.
>
> —*A Million Little Miracles*

The only way to reconcile bad things happening to good people is by adding eternity to the equation. Followers of Jesus believe in something bigger and better—a happily *forever* after.

God is bigger and better than the bad things that have happened to us. Although I wouldn't choose pain and heartache, grief has increased my capacity for joy. The same can be true for you.

Have you found meaning in pain and suffering? How?

_____

_____

_____

_____

_____

_____

_____

_____

_____

> Life is never made unbearable by circumstances, but only by lack of meaning.
>
> —VIKTOR FRANKL[1]

All of us are guilty of affective forecasting. It's the
phenomenon whereby we misjudge what will make us
happy. It's wanting the wrong thing for the right reason
or the right thing for the wrong reason.

—*A Million Little Miracles*

What do we do when bad things happen to us? We ask God
to change our *circumstances*. If that doesn't work, our next
prayer is to ask God to change *others*.

When was the last time you asked God to change *you*?

If you prayed this, what would you ask God to change?

_____

_____

_____

_____

_____

_____

_____

_____

_____

_____

_____

_____

_____

When the world pushes against you, what do you do? Do you draw strength from the Holy Spirit?

Are you being conformed to the world around you, or are you being transformed by the Spirit of God within you?

Enjoy today and don't focus on or worry about tomorrow. Enjoy the journey! No matter how big the problem, God is bigger still.

God is gooder than anything that goes wrong!

Are you being tossed to and fro by *trending hashtags*?
Or are you *shifting the atmosphere* with faith, hope, and love?

—*A Million Little Miracles*

THE SIMPLE SEED

One of God's smallest yet most
amazing miracles is the seed.
—*A Million Little Miracles*

How often do you think of seeds? We can easily take them for granted until we run out of an ingredient like cumin or sesame seeds that a recipe calls for.

Consider a single seed. Just like a single cell, a single drop of water, and a single grain of sand, a seed is definitely not as simple as it seems!

It is more miraculous than we can imagine.

Write down any thoughts you have about seeds, such as your favorite seeds or when you last held a seed.

_____

_____

_____

_____

_____

Then God said, "Let the land sprout with vegetation—every sort of seed-bearing plant, and trees that grow seed-bearing fruit. These seeds will then produce the kinds of plants and trees from which they came." And that is what happened.

—GENESIS I:II, NLT

Seeds—and the process that allows for reproduction—
sustain human life as we know it.

—*A Million Little Miracles*

Think about a watermelon seed. It may be just a little black seed, but it's incredible what that little seed eventually turns into! If that's not a miracle, I'm not sure what is!

Think about other seeds—pumpkin seeds, poppy seeds, sunflower seeds.

What are some tiny seeds planted in your lifetime that you have seen grow into a sizable miracle?

_____

_____

_____

_____

_____

_____

_____

_____

_____

_____

When you can explain to me the mystery of a watermelon, you can ask me to explain the mystery of God.

—WILLIAM JENNINGS BRYAN[1]

When God stepped back at the end of day three and saw
that it was good, it also tasted good.

—*A Million Little Miracles*

When you hear the word "vanilla," what comes to mind?
Sometimes it is used to describe something that lacks special
or extra features. But vanilla is one of the most popular spices
in the world, and plain vanilla is anything but plain. It was
once a rare luxury before the secret to pollinating vanilla
plants was discovered.

What are some ordinary and plain things in your life that
are easy to take for granted?

_____

_____

_____

_____

_____

_____

_____

_____

_____

_____

_____

Every seed is a miracle unto itself, and each one can be traced to the third day of creation. Each is a unique expression of God's goodness.

How often do we overlook these tiny miracles in our daily lives? The next time you pull something off your spice rack or you enjoy a delicious meal, praise God for each of the ingredients.

_____

_____

_____

_____

_____

_____

_____

_____

_____

_____

_____

_____

Go ahead and give your compliments to the chef, but throw in a thank you to the Creator for the raw materials that made the meal possible!

—*A Million Little Miracles*

CHASING BUTTERFLIES

It's chasing butterflies, not catching them, that brings joy.
—A Million Little Miracles

When I picture Adam and Eve, I imagine them before the fall, romping around Eden with butterfly nets in hand.

Imagine how much fun they had!

Imagine what joy that must have brought to the heart of a good God who delights in His playfellows.

What are some things about you that God delights in?

_____

_____

_____

_____

_____

_____

_____

_____

The LORD delights in those who fear him,
who put their hope in his unfailing love.

—PSALM 147:11

Why did God create butterflies? Perhaps it's for
no more noble purpose than play, so kids have
something beautiful to chase.

—*A Million Little Miracles*

Did you know that the monarch butterfly is the only species
of butterfly that migrates like birds do? When the weather
turns cold, they migrate to warmer places.

What is fascinating is that it takes three generations for
monarchs to make the three-thousand-mile journey north
and it takes one generation to make the migration south.[1]

Why do monarchs do this, and how do they know where
to go? This is one of those wonderful mysteries and miracles
of nature that makes life a little more meaningful.

What are some mysteries and miracles of nature that mean
something to you?

_____

_____

_____

_____

_____

I was by his side, a master craftsman,
delighting him day after day,
ever at play in his presence,
at play everywhere in his world,
delighting to be with the sons of men.

—MATTHEW FOX[2]

The journey is the destination, if you enjoy the journey.

—*A Million Little Miracles*

What brings you the most joy in life?

What is your personal version of chasing butterflies?

What makes you feel wild and free?

_____

_____

_____

_____

_____

Counting stars . . .

Considering lilies . . .

Chasing butterflies . . .

Each one is a way of worshipping our Creator.

Remember that God never stops singing and never stops laughing and never stops playing.

_____

_____

_____

_____

The Hebrew word translated "delight" means "laugh" or "play."

—*A Million Little Miracles*

THE DANDELION THEORY

Some children are more sensitive to their circumstances
than others. Then there are children who seem
to flourish against all odds.

—*A Million Little Miracles*

On December 10, 1914, Thomas Edison watched helplessly as his research compound burned to the ground. The fire destroyed much of his lifework. How did Edison respond?

"Thank goodness all our mistakes were burned up," the inventor stated. "Now we can start fresh again."[1]

How would you respond if you saw your lifework suddenly destroyed? What would you do to salvage it?

_____

_____

_____

_____

_____

_____

For I am about to do something new.
    See, I have already begun! Do you not see it?
I will make a pathway through the wilderness.
    I will create rivers in the dry wasteland.

—ISAIAH 43:19, NLT

When we delight in nature, we are doing
what God Himself did.

—*A Million Little Miracles*

A professor who studied stress for four decades came up with
the orchid and the dandelion theory.[2] Children can be like an
orchid, which needs an ideal environment to thrive, or they
can be more like dandelions, flourishing against all odds.

What are you more like—an orchid or a dandelion? Why?

_____

_____

_____

_____

_____

_____

_____

_____

_____

_____

_____

Without wonder, your life is ruled by cynicism, stress,
worry, and anxiety.

—HARRIS III[3]

Wonder can be resurrected in many ways.

—*A Million Little Miracles*

Dandelions are resilient in the face of adversity. So how can we be more resilient in our lives? How can we better deal with the stress and anxieties we face every day?

Maybe your life has become too routine.

Maybe you've lost your wonder for life.

Maybe it's time for a reset.

Where are you when it comes to this?

_____

_____

_____

_____

_____

_____

_____

_____

_____

_____

_____

_____

_____

_____

Do you delight in the present moment? Use curiosity and playfulness as a superpower! Find delight in everything you see and hear and touch.

Flourish against the odds. Don't let routine prevent you from growing.

_____

_____

_____

_____

_____

_____

_____

_____

_____

_____

_____

_____

The plant kingdom is part of this symphony called creation and it never stops singing.

—*A Million Little Miracles*

NAMING RIGHTS

I believe there will be animals in heaven.
Why would there not be?

—*A Million Little Miracles*

One of my favorite moments in all of Scripture is in Genesis when Adam named the animals. Can you picture that moment?

"Adam, I want you to name the animals."

"Which ones?"

"All of them."

It's almost like God was waiting with bated breath to see what Adam would name each animal.

What are some of your favorite animal names? Look up some unfamiliar names and write them down.

_____

_____

_____

_____

Now the Lord God had formed out of the ground all the wild animals and all the birds in the sky. He brought them to the man to see what he would name them; and whatever the man called each living creature, that was its name.

—GENESIS 2:19

Are we having fun yet?
I wouldn't be surprised if that is an actual question God
asked Adam after many days of naming animals.

—A Million Little Miracles

Every animal is a unique testament to God's creativity and goodness. They inspire awe and provide food—and some even make great pets!

If you've had pets, think of your favorite and write down the reasons why they were your favorite. Now think of the most impressive, unique, or creative animal God made. What makes that animal so amazing?

Kings could not obtain a greater honor than to be God's playfellows in that game.

—SIR FRANCIS BACON[1]

When God gave Adam the privilege of naming
the animals, it set the stage for naming
anything and everything.

—A Million Little Miracles

It is easy to read right over the responsibility given to us to name things. It was man's very first job after gardening.

Just as God puts His name on us, we put names on the rest of creation. Naming is a privilege.

Even though your parents gave you a name, your true name won't be revealed until you enter heaven.[2]

Do you consider it a privilege to name things on earth? What do you think your new name might mean?

_____

_____

_____

_____

_____

_____

_____

_____

_____

_____

_____

_____

What if God revealed to you who you are at the deepest level? Suddenly everything would make perfect sense!

Ah—that's *what I am. That makes sense now.*

Picture what that will be like. Our life will flash before our eyes like a composite picture. We will finally see as we are seen!

Today, count your blessings by naming all the miracles you see, from the smallest seed to the largest of galaxies and everything in between!

_____

_____

_____

_____

_____

_____

_____

_____

_____

_____

_____

_____

Whoever names the most miracles wins the gratitude game!

—*A Million Little Miracles*

CHILDLIKENESS

Jesus releases the inner child in all of us!
—A Million Little Miracles

Do you play the shame game? That's feeling bad about who you are. It's a negative feedback loop that says, *I'm not good enough* or *I'm not strong enough* or one of a dozen other deficiencies.

Guilt is different from shame. Guilt is when you admit you made a mistake, while shame claims you *are* a mistake.

Do you have triggers that make you feel unworthy and unwanted in life? What are they?

_____

_____

_____

_____

_____

_____

_____

For we are God's handiwork, created in Christ Jesus to do good works, which God prepared in advance for us to do.

—EPHESIANS 2:10

> Just as pain is an indicator of a physical problem,
> guilt is often an indicator of a spiritual problem.
>
> —*A Million Little Miracles*

How do we win the shame game? The same way we rewrite any negative narrative:

Scripture!

We answer those shame scripts that run in our head with Scripture.

Shame tells you you're a mistake, but God says you are His workmanship.

Shame tells you you're unworthy, but God says you are worth the cross.

What Scripture can answer the shame script that you have in your head?

_____

_____

_____

_____

_____

_____

> If I want to know who I really am and what God intended me to be, I must go back behind the lost paradise, I must look to the morning of creation and try to hear the first words that God spoke to me and my father Adam.
>
> —HELMUT THIELICKE[1]

To become like Jesus is to become like a little child.

—*A Million Little Miracles*

In Matthew 18:3, Jesus says, "Truly I tell you, unless you change and become like little children, you will never enter the kingdom of heaven."

This is one of the most kaleidoscopic statements in all of Scripture.

At the heart of this verse is a call to childlike wonder, childlike curiosity, and childlike playfulness.

What does Matthew 18:3 mean to you? How can you become more childlike?

_____

_____

_____

_____

_____

_____

_____

_____

_____

_____

_____

Repentance doesn't just result in forgiveness. By faith, it flips the wonder switch back on! We start seeing everyone and everything as wonder-full.

We have to stop playing the shame game in our lives. Instead, we need to become like a little child again. To see everyone and everything as redeemable.

Childlikeness and Christlikeness are two sides of the same coin.

—*A Million Little Miracles*

IT'S A WONDERFUL LIFE

None of us chooses when or where we are born.
We don't choose our family of origin or a thousand
other things. We do, however, choose our response
to the challenges life throws at us.

—*A Million Little Miracles*

Life can knock you down and kick dirt in your face. And that's the best time for the Enemy to add insult to injury.

But you can flip the script!

You get to choose how you respond.

You get to see the beauty and goodness that surround you.

You get to believe that you really do have a wonderful life.

How do you respond to those times you've been knocked down? Do you allow the Enemy's voice to discourage you, or do you mute his lies? Write down your thoughts.

_____

_____

_____

_____

_____

Sing to him a new song;
  play skillfully, and shout for joy.

—PSALM 33:3

It's our outlook on life that will determine the outlook of
our life—outlook makes us or breaks us.

—*A Million Little Miracles*

Does the evil in this world ever overwhelm you? Do all the
wrong things in life make you question what is right?

What is your response to the darkness? Are you able to see
God and trust Him in the middle of struggles?

_____

_____

_____

_____

_____

_____

_____

_____

_____

_____

_____

Your destiny can't be changed, but it can be challenged.

—MARTIN HEIDEGGER[1]

We praise God on good days and bad days.

—*A Million Little Miracles*

You can't control your circumstances, but you can challenge them by worshipping through them.

How do you worship like this?

By having childlike wonder.

By counting stars and considering lilies and chasing butterflies.

By giving God your full attention and your full affection.

List ways you can worship God in your life.

_____

_____

_____

_____

_____

_____

_____

_____

_____

_____

_____

_____

_____

"The goodness of God is not a magic wand that we wave over a problem to see it fixed," said Bill Johnson. "It is the context in which we do life. Everything we see and experience is defined by that one prevailing reality: God is good."[2]

Praise God today even if you've been knocked down.

Praise Him because He is holy and worthy.

Praise Him because He is God Most High, God Most Nigh, and God Most Good.

You can't *not* worship! Why? Because the heartbeat of God is imprinted on each of us. We were made by God, for God.

—*A Million Little Miracles*

TRUE WORSHIP

---

*I put songs on repeat because it helps them
sink into my soul.*

—*A Million Little Miracles*

What is the playlist to the soundtrack of your life? Whose voice are you listening to? Is it the loudest? Or is it the still, small voice of the Holy Spirit?

We all have songs that play in our heads. Sometimes they shame and blame us. Other times it is the voice of the One who rejoices over us with singing.

What is the soundtrack to your life? What songs are on your soul's playlist?

_____

_____

_____

_____

_____

The Lord your God is with you,
   the Mighty Warrior who saves.
He will take great delight in you;
   in his love he will no longer rebuke you,
   but will rejoice over you with singing.

—ZEPHANIAH 3:17

Are you building altars to God?
Or are you building monuments to yourself?
The choice is yours, but it's one or the other!

—*A Million Little Miracles*

There are two verses that show the defining moments in King Saul's life. In 1 Samuel 14:35, it says, "Then Saul built an altar to the LORD; it was the first time he had done this."

Saul was giving credit where credit was due. But that changed just one chapter later in 1 Samuel 15:12 when Saul went to the town of Carmel to set up a monument to himself.

Why did Saul start building monuments to himself? I believe he was listening to the wrong song! He let his injured ego get the best of him.

What altars for God have you built in your life? Have you built any monuments to yourself?

_____

_____

_____

_____

_____

_____

The Christian shoemaker does his duty not by putting little crosses on his shoes, but by making good shoes, because God is interested in good craftsmanship.

—MARTIN LUTHER[1]

If you worship God by building altars, your world
gets bigger and bigger and bigger.

—*A Million Little Miracles*

You can worship God in a million ways!

You can run for God.

You can cook for God.

You can write for God.

You don't have to be an Olympian or a gourmet chef or a
published author to do those things!

In what unique ways do you worship God?

_____

_____

_____

_____

_____

_____

_____

_____

_____

_____

_____

_____

_____

_____

_____

There is nothing you have—time, talent, or treasure—that isn't a gift from almighty God. Worship is giving it back to God by giving it all you've got.

So how do we worship in truth?

By keeping that holy curiosity! It's the kind that keeps seeking, asking, and knocking.

_____

_____

_____

_____

_____

_____

_____

_____

_____

_____

_____

When we worship, we aren't just singing. We are *singing back* to the God who rejoices over us with singing, the God who sings songs of deliverance all around us all the time.[2] When we worship, we are harmonizing with heaven.

—*A Million Little Miracles*

EVERY GRAIN OF SAND

Every grain of sand is one of a million little miracles that
we can either take for granted or take for gratitude.
The choice is yours!

—*A Million Little Miracles*

When was the last time you thanked God for a grain of sand?
Maybe you praised Him for being at the beach, but what
about the sand you were lounging on?

Sand is another one of those everyday miracles we take for
granted.

Think about the importance of concrete. We harvest fifty
billion tons of sand every year for construction projects all
over the world![1]

Spend some time thinking about sand and what it means
to you. Describe a beach vacation or maybe the last time you
were on a construction site.

How precious are your thoughts about me, O God.
  They cannot be numbered!
I can't even count them;
  they outnumber the grains of sand!
And when I wake up,
  you are still with me!

—PSALM 139:17–18, NLT

Life is beautiful, but beauty is in the eye of the beholder!
—*A Million Little Miracles*

This journal has been about noticing and thanking God for all the miracles that surround us. So how do you steward a miracle? You do it by believing God for bigger and better miracles.

But you have to do something before you do that.

It all starts with appreciating the miracles that stare you in the face. And of course, that includes the miracle in the mirror—the reflection of the image of God in you.

Do you appreciate all the miracles right in front of you? Especially the one staring at you in the mirror?

I've got miracles on miracles
A million little miracles
—ELEVATION WORSHIP AND MAVERICK CITY MUSIC[2]

Next time you're sitting on a beach, praise God for a
million little miracles between your toes.

—*A Million Little Miracles*

How do you praise God throughout the day?

How can you praise Him when you wake up?

How do you praise Him on your way to work?

How do you praise God throughout the busyness and the
mundane, the happy moments and the sad ones?

_____

_____

_____

_____

_____

_____

_____

_____

_____

_____

_____

_____

_____

How are you feeling as you near the end of this forty-day miracle journey? Do you feel smaller? Does God feel bigger and closer and gooder to you than before you began?

Always remember that you are seen and heard and loved by almighty God. His thoughts toward you outnumber all the sand on all the shores on earth.

Whether we're counting stars, considering lilies, or chasing butterflies, there is a God to thank for His many splendored gifts. He hung the stars, formed the flowers, and created the caterpillars.

—A Million Little Miracles

NOSTALGIA FOR GOD

What's *really* happening when what's happening
is happening?
—*A Million Little Miracles*

Despite the million little miracles we get to see every day, this world is not our home.

Deep down inside all of us, we know from whence we came. Our deepest longing is to find our way back to Eden, where we once walked with God. This longing for Eden will be fulfilled by the second Eden, which the Bible calls heaven.

Do you feel at home in this world? Do you feel a longing for another home, another place?

_____

_____

_____

_____

_____

_____

Surely your goodness and love will follow me
    all the days of my life,
and I will dwell in the house of the LORD
    forever.

—PSALM 23:6

It's not only God's mercies that are new every morning.
It's His miracles! Every day, without exception, we
experience miracles big and small, visible and invisible,
tangible and intangible.

—*A Million Little Miracles*

This longing for Eden is not a place—it's a Person. We long
for the Creator who formed us in His image. Pope Francis
called it "nostalgia for God."[1]

So what do you do with that nostalgia for God?

Remember who God truly is.

How is God bigger than big?

How is God closer than close?

How is God gooder than good?

Write down the things you've learned throughout this
journey.

_____

_____

_____

_____

_____

_____

_____

If I find in myself a desire which no experience in this
world can satisfy, the most probable explanation is that
I was made for another world.

—C. S. LEWIS[2]

The goodness of God has been pursuing you since
the day you [were born], and it will pursue you
until the day you die.

—*A Million Little Miracles*

We may think we're seeking God, but here's the truth:

God is the one seeking us! And He doesn't do this passively or passive-aggressively! He pursues us with more pathos than we've ever experienced!

How have you seen God pursue you?

_____

_____

_____

_____

_____

_____

_____

_____

_____

_____

_____

_____

_____

_____

God has always been pursuing you. Now it's time to return the favor!

Today, seek the God who is seeking you.

Rediscover the God who is bigger than big, closer than close, and gooder than good.

_____

_____

_____

_____

_____

_____

_____

_____

_____

_____

_____

_____

_____

_____

_____

_____

Keep counting stars.
Keep considering lilies.
Keep chasing butterflies.
    —A Million Little Miracles

NOTES

How to Use This Journal

1. Josh Hoffman, "Why Jim Carrey Wrote Himself a $10-Million Check Before He Had $10 Million," Medium, January 7, 2019, https://socialmediajosh.medium.com/why-jim-carrey-wrote-himself-a-10-million-check-before-he-had-10-million-3618090c9e.

Day 1: Holy Curiosity

1. Einstein is credited for this quote. See "Albert Einstein: Quotes," Goodreads, accessed June 4, 2024, www.goodreads.com/quotes/987-there-are-only-two-ways-to-live-your-life-one.
2. G. K. Chesterton, *Orthodoxy* (Dodd, Mead & Co., 1908; repr., Moody, 2009), 36–37.

Day 2: Baptism by Nature

1. John Muir, *Selected Writings* (Alfred A. Knopf, 2017), 271.
2. Henry David Thoreau, "Thoreau's Journal (Part IV)," *Atlantic,* April 1905, www.theatlantic.com/magazine/archive/1905/04/thoreaus-journal-part-iv/542109.

Day 3: Ask the Earth and It Will Teach You

1. George Washington Carver, *George Washington Carver: In His Own Words,* ed. G. R. Kremer (University of Missouri Press, 1987), 142–43.

Day 4: Goosebumps

1. Psalm 34:3, BSB.
2. Karl Rahner, paraphrased by Ron Rolheiser, "Divine Providence," RonRohleiser.com, January 24, 1999, https://ronrolheiser.com/divine-providence.

Day 5: Neoteny

1. Dr. Seuss is credited with this quote. See TJ McCue, "Six Lessons from Dr. Seuss," *Forbes,* January 1, 2013, https://www.forbes.com/sites/tjmccue/2013/01/01/6-lessons-from-dr-seuss/.
2. C. S. Lewis, *Letters to Malcolm: Chiefly on Prayer* (Harcourt Brace Jovanovich, 1964), 93.
3. Walt Disney, *The Quotable Walt Disney,* comp. Dave Smith (Disney Editions, 2001), Google Books.

Day 6: Tov

1. Fyodor Dostoevsky, *The Idiot,* trans. Richard Pevear and Larissa Volokhonsky (Vintage Classics, 2001), 382.

Day 7: Kabash

1. G. K. Chesterton, *Orthodoxy* (Dodd, Mead & Co., 1908; repr., Moody, 2009), 144.

Day 8: Kedushah

1. Abraham Joshua Heschel, *God in Search of Man: A Philosophy of Judaism* (Farrar, Straus and Giroux, 1955), 46.

2. Heschel, *God in Search of Man,* 46.

3. Westminster Shorter Catechism, Q & A 1.

Day 9: The Infinitude of God

1. Genesis 15:5.

2. A. W. Tozer, *The Knowledge of the Holy* (HarperOne, 1978), 46–47.

Day 11: Reality Distortion Field

1. See Psalm 46:1.

2. See Hebrews 13:8.

3. See Exodus 3:14.

4. Oswald Chambers, "Inspired Invincibility," *My Utmost for His Highest,* accessed April 14, https://utmost.org/classic/inspired -invincibility-classic.

5. John Ortberg, *If You Want to Walk on Water, You've Got to Get Out of the Boat* (Zondervan, 2001).

Day 12: God Winks

1. A.W. Tozer, *The Knowledge of the Holy* (HarperOne, 1978), 47.

Day 13: A Single Drop of Water

1. A mole is a unit of measurement used to describe the amounts of reactants and products of chemical reactions. Wikipedia, s.v. "Avogadro constant," last modified May 4, 2024, https://en .wikipedia.org/wiki/Avogadro_constant.

2. Wilson Bentley, quoted in "Wilson A. Bentley (1865–1931),"

Snowflake Bentley, accessed May 4, 2024, https://snowflake
bentley.com/biography.

3. See Isaiah 49:16.

Day 14: Gratitude Lists

1. Robert Brault, quoted in Madhuleena Roy Chowdhury, "The
Neuroscience of Gratitude and Effects on the Brain," Positive-
Psychology, September 19, 2024, https://positivepsychology
.com/neuroscience-of-gratitude/.

Day 15: Study the Ant

1. "13 Fun Fact About Camels," SPANA, accessed May 4, 2024,
https://spana.org/blog/13-fun-facts-about-camels.

2. Rebecca Dzombak, "How Many Ants Are There on Earth?
You're Going to Need More Zeros," *New York Times,* September 22, 2022, www.nytimes.com/2022/09/22/science/ants
-census-20-quadrillion.html.

3. Patrick Schultheiss, quoted in Dzombak, "How Many Ants?"

4. Fyodor Dostoevsky, "Fyodor Dostoevsky: Quotes," Goodreads,
accessed May 4, 2024, www.goodreads.com/quotes/126038
-every-ant-knows-the-formula-of-its-ant-hill-every-bee.

Day 16: Stabs of Joy

1. C. S. Lewis, *Surprised by Joy: The Shape of My Early Life* (Harper
One, 2017), 6.

2. C. S. Lewis, *Surprised by Joy,* 6.

3. Ramakrishna Akula and Soumya Mukherjee, "New Insights
on Neurotransmitters Signaling Mechanisms in Plants," *Plant
Signaling & Behavior* 15, no. 6 (2020), https://doi.org/10.1080/
15592324.2020.1737450.

Day 18: Choose Your Miracle

1. Glen Scrivener, quoted in Rebecca McLaughlin, *Is Christmas Unbelievable? Four Questions Everyone Should Ask About the World's Most Famous Story* (The Good Book Company, 2021), 45.
2. Zeeshan Ahmed et al., "Human Gene and Disease Associations for Clinical-Genomics and Precision Medicine Research," *Clinical and Translational Medicine* 10, no. 1 (2020): 297–318, https://doi.org/10.1002/ctm2.28.
3. Fred Hoyle, quoted in Ron Carlson and Ed Decker, *Fast Facts on False Teachings* (Harvest House, 1994), 57.

Day 19: Extrasensory Perception

1. Tim Jewell, "Tetrachromacy ('Super Vision')," Healthline, updated December 21, 2023, https://www.healthline.com/health/tetrachromacy.
2. Marcel Proust, *The Captive and the Fugitive,* vol. 5 of *In Search of Lost Time,* trans. C. K. Scott Moncrieff, ed. William C. Carter (Yale University Press, 2023), 764.

Day 20: Heavenly Frequency

1. Thomas Carlyle, "The Opera," in Lewis Worthington Smith, *The Mechanism of English Style* (Oxford University Press, 1916), 101.
2. C. S. Lewis, *Reflections on the Psalms* (Harcourt, 1958), 94.

Day 21: The Wonder Switch

1. Monica Parker, *The Power of Wonder: The Extraordinary Emotion That Will Change the Way You Live, Learn, and Lead* (TarcherPerigee, 2023), 9.

2. Harris III, *The Wonder Switch: The Difference Between Limiting Your Life and Living Your Dream* (Zondervan Thrive, 2020), 3–4.

3. Robert McCammon, *Boy's Life* (Pocket Books, 1991), 2.

4. Thomas Carlyle, *On Heroes, Hero-Worship, and the Heroic in History* (James Fraser, 1866), 8.

Day 22: The Dandelion Principle

1. G. K. Chesterton, *Autobiography* (Hutchinson & Company, 1936), 95.

Day 23: Imagination Is Everything

1. John Lloyd and John Mitchinson, *The Book of General Ignorance* (Harmony Books, 2006), xx.

2. "Grasshopper Long Jump," Randall Museum, https://randall museum.org/wp-content/uploads/olympics-long-jump.pdf.

3. "Science: The Grasshopper's Hop," *Time,* January 6, 1958, https://time.com/archive/6805707/science-the-grasshoppers -hop/.

4. Franz Kafka, "Franz Kafka: Quotes," Goodreads, accessed May 6, 2024, www.goodreads.com/quotes/18883-you-do-not -need-to-leave-your-room-remain-sitting.

Day 24: Imaginarium of Tears

1. Maurice Mikkers, "The Journey of Imaginarium of Tears," Medium, January 7, 2016, https://medium.com/micrograph -stories/the-journy-of-imaginarium-of-tears-5f70c8fb6f53.

Day 25: The Loneliness Epidemic

1. Genesis 2:18.

Day 26: Gooder Than Good

1. C. S. Lewis, *The Lion, the Witch and the Wardrobe* (Harper Collins, 2005), 80.
2. See Proverbs 9:10.

Day 27: A Progressive Revelation

1. A. W. Tozer, *The Knowledge of the Holy* (General Press, 2019), chap. 16, ebook.

Day 28: Name Above All Names

1. "What are the different names of God, and what do they mean?," Got Questions, accessed February 3, 2025, https://www.gotquestions.org/names-of-God.html.
2. Sally Lloyd-Jones, *The Jesus Storybook Bible: Every Story Whispers His Name* (Zonderkidz, 2007), 17.
3. See John 6:35; 8:12; 10:9, 11; 11:25; 14:6; 15:1.
4. Eugene Peterson, *Christ Plays in Ten Thousand Places: A Conversation in Spiritual Theology* (Wm. B. Eerdmans, 2005), 103.

Day 29: Goodwill Toward Men

1. See 2 Corinthians 3:18, KJV.
2. C. S. Lewis, quoted in C. W. Feldmann, "C. S. Lewis and the Old Testament," God'sCharacter.com, June 15, 2012, www.godscharacter.com/the-god-blog/cs-lewis-and-the-old-testament.
3. See Romans 12:2.

Day 30: The Life Lie

1. C. G. Jung, "Commentary on 'The Secret of the Golden Flower,'" in *Collected Works of C. G. Jung,* vol. 13, *Alchemical Studies,* ed. Gerhard Adler, trans. R.F.C. Hull (Princeton University Press, 1983), 15.

Day 31: Order Out of Chaos

1. Viktor Frankl, quoted in Daisy Grewal, "A Happy Life May Not Be a Meaningful Life," *Scientific American*, February 18, 2014, www.scientificamerican.com/article/a-happy-life-may -not-be-a-meaningful-life.

Day 32: The Simple Seed

1. William Jennings Bryan, quoted in "Watermelon," Bible.org, February 2, 2009, https://bible.org/illustration/watermelon.

Day 33: Chasing Butterflies

1. "Migration and Overwintering," U.S. Forest Service, accessed April 15, 2025, https://www.fs.usda.gov/wildflowers/pollina tors/Monarch_Butterfly/migration/index.shtml.
2. Matthew Fox, *Original Blessing: A Primer in Creation Spirituality Presented in Four Paths, Twenty-Six Themes, and Two Questions* (Bear, 1983; repr., Tarcher, 2000), 37.

Day 34: The Dandelion Theory

1. Thomas Edison, "Thomas Edison: Quotes," Goodreads, accessed May 25, 2024, www.goodreads.com/quotes/7554496 -when-thomas-edison-s-factory-burned-to-the-ground-in -1914.

2. Dave Davies, "Is Your Child an Orchid or a Dandelion? Unlocking the Science of Sensitive Kids," NPR, March 4, 2019, www.npr.org/sections/health-shots/2019/03/04/699979387/is-your-child-an-orchid-or-a-dandelion-unlocking-the-science-of-sensitive-kids.

3. Harris III, *The Wonder Switch: The Difference Between Limiting Your Life and Living Your Dream* (Zondervan Thrive, 2020), 3.

Day 35: Naming Rights

1. Francis Bacon, *The Works of Francis Bacon,* vol. 6, ed. James Spedding et al. (Houghton Mifflin, 1904), 141.

2. See Isaiah 62:2; Revelation 2:17.

Day 36: Childlikeness

1. Helmut Thielicke, *How the World Began: Man in the First Chapters of the Bible,* trans. John Doberstein (Fortress, 1961), 7.

Day 37: It's a Wonderful Life

1. Martin Heidegger, "Martin Heidegger: Quotes," Goodreads, accessed May 26, 2024, www.goodreads.com/author/quotes/6191.Martin_Heidegger.

2. Bill Johnson, *God Is Good: He's Better Than You Think,* rev. ed. (Destiny Image, 2018), 225.

Day 38: True Worship

1. "Martin Luther: Quotes," Goodreads, www.goodreads.com/author/quotes/29874.Martin_Luther.

2. See Psalm 32:7; Zephaniah 3:17.

Day 39: Every Grain of Sand

1. "The Problem with Our Dwindling Sand Reserves," United Nations Environment Programme, February 6, 2023, www.unep.org/news-and-stories/story/problem-our-dwindling-sand-reserves.

2. Elevation Worship and Maverick City Music, "Million Little Miracles," track 6 on *Old Church Basement,* Elevation Worship and Provident Label Group, 2021.

Day 40: Nostalgia for God

1. Francis, "Nostalgia for God," The Holy See, October 1, 2015, www.vatican.va/content/francesco/en/cotidie/2015/documents/papa-francesco-cotidie_20151001_nostalgia-for-god.html.

2. C. S. Lewis, *Mere Christianity* (HarperOne, 2001), 136–37.

ABOUT THE AUTHOR

MARK BATTERSON is the lead pastor of National Community Church (national.cc) in Washington, DC. One church in multiple locations, National owns and operates Ebenezers Coffeehouse, the DC Dream Center, and the Capital Turnaround. Mark holds a doctor of ministry degree from Regent University and is the *New York Times* bestselling author of twenty-five books, including *The Circle Maker, Chase the Lion,* and *Win the Day.* He also authored the children's books *The Best Worst Day Ever* and *God Speaks in Whispers* with his daughter, Summer Batterson Dailey. Mark Batterson and his wife, Lora, live on Capitol Hill in Washington, DC.

Also from bestselling author
MARK BATTERSON

Be reminded of the millions of miracles God performs every day, and be inspired to live with a clearer sense of identity and purpose.

Dig into the Bible with this compelling companion study guide. Engage with key questions and activities and note the ways God reveals His greatness and reminds us of His goodness.

MULTNOMAH

Learn more about Mark Batterson's books at waterbrookmultnomah.com.